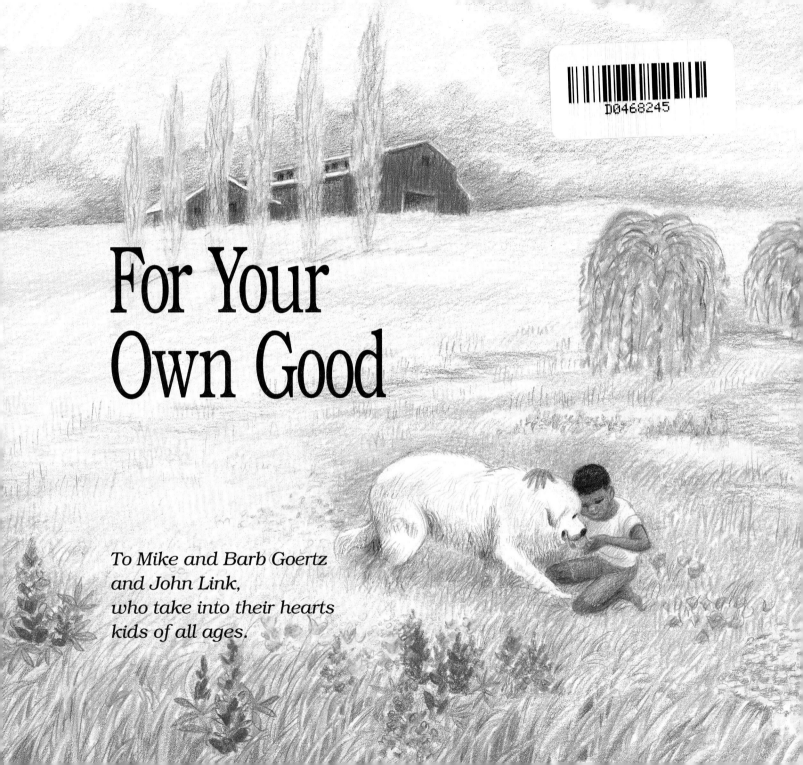

For Your Own Good

To Mike and Barb Goertz
and John Link,
*who take into their hearts
kids of all ages.*

It began one night last summer. Actually, it didn't begin then at all. In some ways it ENDED then. But I had better start from the beginning and explain.

Jamin and me was left alone at home while my mom and her boyfriend Jake were out doin' drugs. It didn't matter, really. I knew how to take care of my little brother.

When my mom and Jake came home drunk, Jake starts beatin' me up. It's happened lots of times

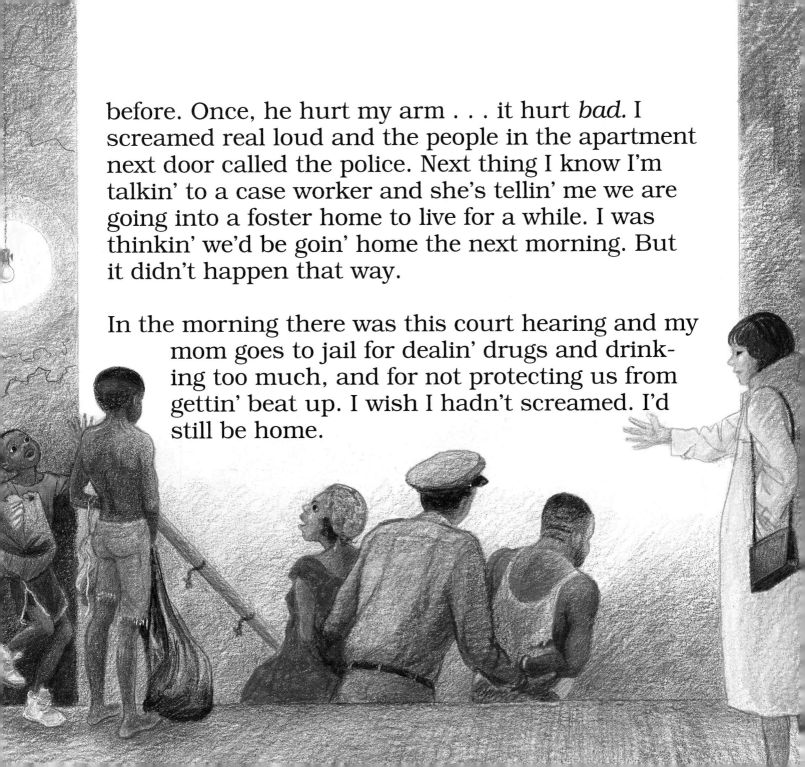

before. Once, he hurt my arm . . . it hurt *bad.* I screamed real loud and the people in the apartment next door called the police. Next thing I know I'm talkin' to a case worker and she's tellin' me we are going into a foster home to live for a while. I was thinkin' we'd be goin' home the next morning. But it didn't happen that way.

In the morning there was this court hearing and my mom goes to jail for dealin' drugs and drinking too much, and for not protecting us from gettin' beat up. I wish I hadn't screamed. I'd still be home.

Teddy leaned in close and licked me right smack in the face. It's like he was tryin' to say, "Living away from your family is hard, no matter why you gotta do it. You did a good thing in screaming. It might force your mom to know she has a problem. Staying around to get beat up was not the only thing you could do, but you didn't know that then."

So here I am, livin' with two grownups and a bunch of kids I don't know. Teddy, I don't even know what to call them. Everybody else calls 'em Mom and Dad. They're not MY mom and dad! They said I could call them Bob and Nancy. I'm tryin' to do

everything right so I don't
make nobody mad. My mom
is going to stop doin' drugs
and drinking and then I'll go
home. Probably next week.

This is really a weird place. All the kids have to take a bath every night and the whole family eats together at the kitchen table. I wonder when they will run out of food and we will be hungry, like at home. I'm not sleepin' in pajamas at night, no matter WHAT their rules are.

"Hey, Cassie, I don't like it when people ask me how come my parents didn't want me. You ask me that again and I'll punch you out!"

I'd no sooner said it than there was Bob. I figured this was it. I was gong to get hit good this time. But it didn't happen! Bob said, "TIME OUT, Jerome," and sent me to my room. That was it. I never DID get beat!

When I was on my bed, Bob said, "Being in foster care doesn't make you any better or worse than other kids. You aren't to blame for your mom's problems.

"The next time you feel like hitting somebody, go down by the creek and scream real loud. Don't hit anybody, just scream. We think that you are a good boy and can learn what to do when you are mad."

Bob sat quietly on the floor beside my bed. After a while I said, "What am I spose to say when people ask me where I came from, and why I'm living in a foster home?"

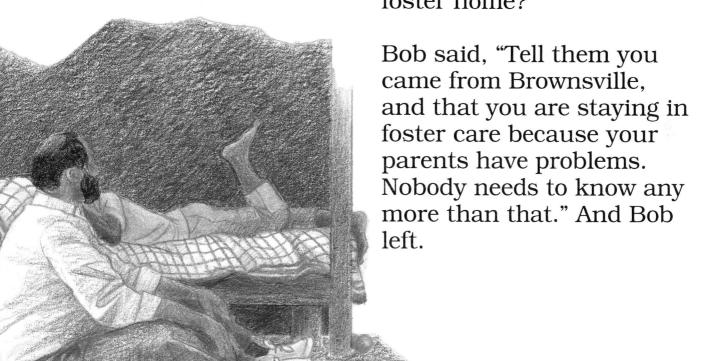

Bob said, "Tell them you came from Brownsville, and that you are staying in foster care because your parents have problems. Nobody needs to know any more than that." And Bob left.

Jamin raced into the room, and the next thing I know he is sittin' in the closet cutting up his new school shirts. Teddy followed him in and Jamin kicked him real hard. When Teddy yelped, Ricky yelled, "I'm tellin!" And the next thing I knew, Nancy was explaining that Jamin would be doing some extra chores to earn the money to pay for new shirts. Starting TODAY.

That night I couldn't sleep. Teddy sneaked in and climbed up on my bed. I could hardly breathe, but I wasn't moving. No way! The nightmares were so scary. Nancy had said to make up a happy ending when the bad dreams came. I'm tryin'. When Jamin had nightmares, Nancy lined up all of the stuffed animals around his bed to "stand guard," and put the cuddliest one in bed with him. It made him smile.

The next day me and Jamin were goin' to go to therapy. Nancy said we would talk to a nice man about our feelings. I don't know how to do that. I didn't want to go, but it didn't look like we had much choice. We were goin'! I wasn't going to say nothin' bad about our parents, though!

The therapy room was filled with neat toys and I decided maybe this wouldn't be too bad after all. I remembered the therapist saying, "You might feel sad and angry and hurt and scared. You have a right to those feelings."

Jamin and me got dressed early the morning of our first visit with mom. Mom was living at a place where they help people with drug and alcohol problems. Jake had moved to another apartment and was taking an "Anger Management" class. A lady would drive us to the State office. We were SO excited.

But Mom never showed up. CAN YOU BELIEVE IT? She never even came!

When I got home I told Cory that my mom was in an accident and couldn't get to the office for the visit. Cory said, "I get it; she never showed up, huh?"

I started to hit him, but Cory said, "I'm sorry. It happens to other kids, too. You can't make your mom do the right thing. Only SHE can do that. But when you DO see her, you can tell her how you feel. And you can have a backup plan of something fun to do, in case she doesn't show up the next time."

I headed for the kitchen. I would eat the biggest bowl of ice cream and a whole

package of cookies and . . .
but Teresa was there. For
SURE she would tell. She
LOVED getting other kids in
trouble! I couldn't stand it
anymore. I picked up Jamin's
farm set and threw it across
the room, smashed my fist
into the wall, tore some wall-
paper, and kicked the
furniture. Now Jamin was
screaming. Teresa was
screaming. And I was screaming. When Bob came, I yelled,
"You just take care of foster
kids so you'll get rich. You
don't care about nobody!"

Bob said, "Come on, Jerome, we're going for a walk." Bob was quiet for a while and then he said, "What you DID was not okay, but who you are IS okay." It was hard for me to understand. When we got to the creek, Bob said, "Okay, now try to put it into words. How do you feel?" I tucked my head down on my chest and cried. I didn't KNOW words for this kind of hurt. Teddy sat quietly with his big, furry head on my lap.

When I could talk, I said, "It was Cory's fault." Bob said, "No matter what anyone says to you, you always have choices about how you will respond. You can learn to think before you act."

"Stay here until you feel under control, then come back to the house. We're going skating this afternoon."

"Really, Dad? I never been skating. I probably won't be no good."

"Maybe. Maybe not. Having fun is more important than being GOOD at skating."

I watched Bob run back to the house. I could barely hear him when he yelled to Nancy, "He called me 'Dad!' I think he feels safe here. What a day this has been!"

That night I watched TV. Good thing the couch was soft, after two hours of skating (or in my case, FALLING DOWN). There are SO MANY things I don't know how to do—how to play games with other kids, how to use the silverware at dinner, what to do when we go places together, how to do things on time, how to do chores. Everything is so different here. I wonder if I will EVER learn.

School is hard. The grownups had a meeting to figure out how to help me do better at school. Every day I go to the "Resource Room," where a special teacher helps me. It's hard to sit still. And it's hard to remember what the teacher tells me to do. Some days I mostly daydream.

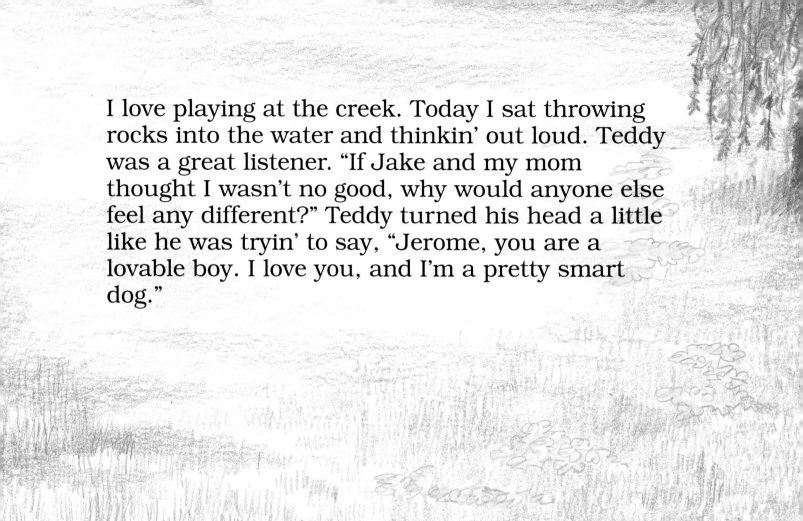

I love playing at the creek. Today I sat throwing rocks into the water and thinkin' out loud. Teddy was a great listener. "If Jake and my mom thought I wasn't no good, why would anyone else feel any different?" Teddy turned his head a little like he was tryin' to say, "Jerome, you are a lovable boy. I love you, and I'm a pretty smart dog."

I know it's been too easy
to blame the way I've been
behavin' on how Mom and
Jake always used to treat
me. My foster parents treat
me like they believe I can do
things RIGHT. They spend
time with me even when I
know they are busy.

Jamin and me have lived in a foster home for one year now. Mom is still doin' drugs, and I know she can't take care of us. We're goin' to live with my aunt and uncle in another state. It's scary to think about leaving this place, but Bob and Nancy say the move won't happen all of a sudden. I HOPE not. They say we can go for weekend visits for several months before we move in with them.

The day is finally here. It's time to go. Jamin and I have been mad at Bob and Nancy lately. Nancy said, "I think it might make you sad to leave this home, and that you might be angry at us for letting it happen. You probably also feel excited to be going to live with your aunt and uncle. You two have been in trouble a lot lately, but lots of kids act that way when it's time to leave. It's okay for you to go. We think you will be happy in your new home."

The kids were outside and ready to wave good-bye. Bob put his arms around me and Jamin and gave us a hug. "We liked having you in our family this year. We think you are GREAT boys!" Jamin said, "Not great, the BEST!" And everyone laughed.

Dear Friend,

Children may live in a variety of family situations when their own biological parents are unable to care for them. Life is not reversible; children cannot *un*-experience what has happened to them. But they can learn to grow from the experience of living with other caregivers.

1. Biological parents may love their children and at the same time be unable to provide safe parenting.

2. If children must choose between abusive biological parents and emotionally healthy foster parents, they will choose their biological parents.

3. Regardless of the reason for foster care, children generally do not perceive it to be "for their own good."

4. Children respond to living in a foster home in various ways. Some children will be on their best behavior initially while they "check out" the new place.

5. The circumstances of the child's removal from home will greatly impact his response to foster care.